DAF LORRIES

BILL REID

AMBERLEY

Acknowledgements

The majority of the photographs in this book are from my own cameras, or from my collection amassed over the years. I would like to thank Pat Crang, Ken Durston, Glen McBirnie, Alex Syme, Bob Tuck, and Eddie Waugh for their assistance and use of photographs.

First published 2017

Amberley Publishing
The Hill, Stroud
Gloucestershire, GL5 4EP

www.amberley-books.com

Copyright © Bill Reid, 2017

The right of Bill Reid to be identified as the Author of this work has been asserted in accordance with the Copyrights, Designs and Patents Act 1988.

ISBN 978 1 4456 6758 4 (print)
ISBN 978 1 4456 6759 1 (ebook)

British Library Cataloguing in Publication Data.
A catalogue record for this book is available from the British Library.

Typesetting by Amberley Publishing.
Printed in the UK.

Introduction

DAF trucks were an unknown quantity in the UK before 1966. The DAF company had been formed by Hub van Doorne as a small engineering company in Holland in 1928. He and his brother, Wim, built up a successful trade in repairs and general engineering, which led to the manufacture of trailers and motor trucks, using the name Van Doorne's Machinefabriek (DAF).

DAF trucks were well-engineered and popular in Holland. Perkins diesel engines were used, and later Leyland designs were fitted in a growing range of trucks and buses.

The name of DAF was virtually unknown in the UK until 1966, when two distributors were set up in England when a perceived shortage of new truck availability was evident. Initial sales were of the then DAF 1800 and 1900 models, which could be used as rigid and articulated types.

However, sales were slow due a lack of dealer support.

The DAFs on offer had a small cab – about the same dimensions as most of the UK types on sale – but the interior was much better than most. That did not help in sales unfortunately, and with the UK transport operators having a very conservative attitude, sales did not open up for a few more years when a better product range was offered. The new range offered in the UK had a wider specification than the early imports, so sales began to rise. Heavier types were also introduced, including the revolutionary cabbed 2600 model, which set the course for later types well into the heavy haulage sphere.

In time DAF trucks in the UK were as popular as any European truck manufacturer's products, with many operators running nothing else. The range was competent, well-powered, and the cabs were comfortable places for the drivers, competing well with other marques.

In the 1980s, the British Leyland truck operation was in danger of collapsing through a lack of funding. In 1986 meetings took place to discuss a merger with Leyland and DAF, which, after many discussions, took place in 1987. Manufacture of DAF trucks began at Leyland, alongside the then Leyland range. Any truck sold in the UK carried Leyland DAF badging.

In the 1990s, DAF had a product in the 95 series – trucks that gained industry awards and saw an upsurge in the company fortunes – but, unfortunately, in 1993 a global recession impacted heavily on the company, which saw bankruptcy being declared.

However, inside a month the Dutch and Belgian governments bailed out the company in the interest of local employment. A new company – DAF Trucks NV – was formed.

In 1996 it was announced that DAF would become part of the US-based PACCAR Inc., which included Kenworth, Peterbilt, and Foden. The amalgamation did not affect DAF production, which was allowed to carry on its business as usual. Foden Trucks were eventually phased out of production in 2005, but not before an adapted DAF cab was fitted to the Foden Alpha range.

Rationalisation of the old British Leyland designs took place and soon all the Leyland-manufactured types were badged as DAFs. An arrangement with Volvo and Renault produced similar cabs for the lightweight and middleweight trucks, with the current DAF range extended from lightweight 7.5-ton lorries to ultra-heavyweight abnormal load tractors, giving a comprehensive coverage right across the needs of the UK transport industry.

Early DAF imports were used by Ackworth Transport from 1966. The cab on the 1800 and 1900 range was not far removed from contemporary British lorries of the time.

A close-up view of a 1967 DAF 1800 unit in the Onward fleet, a subsidiary of Ackworth Transport. The cab was not very modern in appearance, but was well-finished inside. The type was not well-suited to UK haulage and not many were sold.

The larger DAF 2600 with a sleeper cab began to be sold in small number from 1971. It was popular because of the sleeper cab, which was not normally found on trucks sold in the UK at the time. The 2600 was also available as a rigid truck, or as a 6x4 heavy haulage unit. (B. Tuck)

When introduced in 1962, the DAF 2600 was a big step forward in driver accommodation, with seating and insulation that made it one of the most advanced cabs available.

By 1970, DAF had designed and was marketing a new cab, which could be built in a modular fashion, suiting middle-weight chassis, and maximum-weight artic types. It could be built in different lengths and widths. The Onward driver training 2100 shows the style for middle-weights.

Nat Ross Ltd used a 2100 as a furniture van. Like the Onward artic, it carries the large plastic grille. Earlier cab versions had simpler metal grilles. The cab was the first DAF tilting design and a DAF 8.25 litre engine was fitted.

The 2100 with its 230 bhp engine became a popular model in the 16-tonner market, with its higher power. Contemporary UK-built designs were not reaching this power level at the time.

The 2100 range was considered ideal for many uses and Ian McFadzean, of Kirkmichael, used his on livestock removal. It is seen here being washed after hauling cattle into the old Ayr Market.

The 2100 range includes 6x2 and 6x4 types. This one, operated by James Herd of Auchterarder, is a straightforward platform lorry, with the versatility to carry many different types of load. When photographed it had brought vintage tractors to an annual vintage show near Perth.

James A. Sharpe & Co. ran two almost identical 2100 trucks painted up in the traditional Scottish style, with tartan embellishment. This one has been parked up in the old Ayr Market, near Ayr town centre.

F. Davidson was the founder of a cattle and general haulage business, which is in the hands of the third family generation today, using mainly DAFs. This 2100 was used in the 1980s.

Another 2100 being used as a transporter for vintage tractors and machinery, with a small beaver tail for easier loading. At the time of the photograph it was not a show exhibit itself, but could fulfil that duty in the present day.

A 2100 with a refrigerated van body based in Aberdeen, and part of the extensive fish processing business in the city. The higher powered engine would make for faster journey times to the south with fresh fish loads.

A very tidy looking 2100 just about to bolster up the long-standing John Maitland fleet of milk tankers. Maitland always ran their tankers, and previous churn lorries in this smart traditional style with fleet names. The DAF carries 'Souter Johnnie' – a well-known name in a Robert Burns local epic poem.

The DAF 2500 was a higher powered version of the 2100 and was intended for heavier gross weights. This one, used by the Edinburgh Woollen Mill, was fitted out as a drawbar unit and handled demountable bodies, serving the countrywide shopping chain of that name.

The 2500 was capable of running at 32 tonnes gross weight, as seen here with this 4-axle artic tipper. It would have been on the edge of its power range, and was probably not the best lorry to drive fully laden.

A 2500 parked up at the Scottish National Exhibition Centre, in Glasgow, after having delivered exhibition material. The amount of rear axle suspension articulation is evident, as is the good steering lock.

There has always been a market for 8-wheel tippers in the UK, and DAF produced such a chassis in the 2500 range. With the smaller 8.25-litre engine and lightweight tipping gear, it probably was able to take a good 20-tonne load, within its 32-tonne GVW.

The wide version of the tilt cab was first seen in 1970, fitted to the 2800 heavyweight models. It is seem here on a James McBride curtainsider of the 1980s. DAF did not make radical changes to their cabs over long periods.

The DAF 2800 became a firm favourite in many large fleets during the 1980s. Gross weights could be much higher than the current 32-tonne GTW, making them suitable as heavy haulage tractors, with over 300 bhp on tap.

The 2300 was intended as an artic unit for 28–30 tonnes GTW, and eminently suitable as a local distribution artic with its lower and narrower cab. This one would have a ZF 6-speed gearbox and a 2-speed splitter, to spread the 203 bhp of its 8.25-litre engine. (G. McBirnie collection)

The 2800 was more commonly found in long-distance work, epitomised by this BRS Western general haulage artic. By now drivers had the option to use sleeper cabs, rather than find accommodation, which could vary in many ways. (K. Durston)

For long-distance or trunking work, the DAF 2800 would be a better proposition with a larger engine, cab, and heavier gross height. In this instance the DAF pictured has all these attributes compared with its fleet stablemate in an earlier picture. (G. McBirnie collection)

In the same era, the 2800 became a popular type with livestock removers, with many being seen, as here, with a double-deck cattle trailer, or four decks for sheep.

The 2800 could be rated as a heavy haulage tractor, pulling lowloader trailers at weights well above the normal 32 tonnes. William Speirs of Irvine, Ayrshire, used this one to transport high and wide loads, usually diggers, from site to site.

Stan Robson, the founder of Robson's Border Transport, well-known for naming each truck in the fleet, did not believe in sleeper cabs, so many of the DAFs introduced to the fleet had so-called day cabs. It was unusual to see a DAF 2800 with such a cab, but not at Robson's Distribution Services, as the company became known.

A normal sleeper-cabbed 2800 finished in the traditional Scottish style, complete with an air deflector giving the impression that the cab is much higher. It was attending an Aberdeenshire vintage vehicle rally some years ago as a transporter, but would fit in well today as an exhibit.

The 2800 was superseded by the broadly similar 3300 with a higher powered engine. Turners of Sedgefield took a heavy haulage tractor and converted it to a recovery wagon, which would take most recovery jobs in its stride.

The higher powered DAF 3300 was ideally suited to an uprate of truck weights in the 1980s to 38 tonnes on artics. Patrick Gilhooly used this one at 38 tonnes in the 2+3-axle set-up, which was then the most expensive road tax class (£3,100). 3+2 was cheaper at around £2,500, while 3+3 was charged at £1,300 per annum.

D. J. Dunabie of Maybole, in Ayrshire, had a number of DAFs in their fleet. This 2800 has the rather plain colour scheme they were known for, as far back as denationalisation in the 1950s.

DAF cabs have been used by other truck manufacturers over the years. This very tall adapted version graced a Finnish SISU, and predates the Renault Magnum by a few years.

The 3300 range toppers were heavy haulage tractors and were in high demand during the 1980s. 100-tonne gross weights and above were commonplace during the boom years of open-cast coal mining, and this Cadzow Heavy Haulage example is waiting for a police escort to such a mine.

A Henry Thomson DAF 3300 in more normal 38-tonne specification with a large livestock trailer, awaiting a load in the old Ayr Cattle Market. It would have taken a load of cattle to abattoirs in England, or a load of sheep to France.

DAF adapted the 3300 with a second steering axle to qualify for the UK 38-tonnes GTW, as did other truck manufacturers of the time. Some would have third axle conversions known as tag-axles, or pusher axles, if fitted in front of the drive axle.

This book is mainly about DAF trucks in use by UK operators, but occasionally European operators would appear with something unusual. This 3300 drawbar outfit was in Scotland for a load, and was unusual with a tri-axle rigid drawbar trailer, coupled almost behind the rearmost axle. This set-up was later to become common in the UK, but the cab-top sleeper did not catch on.

West of Scotland Heavy Haulage also used the DAF 3300 as a heavyweight mover, and still use the current DAF types. This one is seen moving a new Terex dump truck, probably to Southampton for export, in an M6 service area.

Another 3300 in traditional Scottish livery, which was used as a heavy haulage unit and as a tipper when needed. The figure in the cab reversing the outfit is George Cunningham, one of the company directors.

Fulton & Semple was a small Ayrshire haulage business with a few trucks on long-distance work. In the main they were DAFs and this fine-looking 3300 was one of the last. The fleet name is *The Grey Maere Meg*, a reference to the Scottish poet Robert Burns' work of *Tam o' Shanter*.

The south-west of Scotland is coal-rich and after the traditional methods of mining closed, tracts of land were taken up for open-cast mining. The DAF 3300 shown here had a GTW of over 100 tonnes and is seem with a large part of a mining machine. It had a police escort and took 3 hours to cover the last 25 miles of its journey.

Well-known in the preservation scene is Geoff Newsome's fleet of preserved lorries. His DAF 3300 represents a 32-tonne artic tipper of the early 1980s, and is seen at the start of an Ayrshire Road Run.

With the advent of heavier gross weights in the UK, DAF introduced the 3600 model –
essentially a higher powered version of the 3300 – just before the unveiling of the new
range of lorries to be known as the 95XF. This one, with 6 axles, was used on scrap metal
haulage.

The higher powered version, the 3600, also appeared as a heavy haulage tractor. Vibro
Heavy Haulage were using their 3600 for STGO Category loads up to 150 tonnes, and had
it converted with the addition of a load-spreading fourth axle on smaller wheels.

The 3300 remained a competent truck at 38 tonnes gross and were in use for many years. Wilson's Transport of Bradford used this one on textile haulage to and from Scotland and it is seen in the town of Kilmarnock, with a well-roped and sheeted load. (A. Syme)

Remaining in the Scottish town of Kilmarnock, this 3300 was used by a local firm of removal contractors. It seems to be a former artic unit, given a long chassis stretch and a very large luton van body. Today, this principle is taken further with the addition of a third axle for higher weights.

The original DAF 2100 was considered a heavyweight 2-axle chassis and there was a call for a lighter chassis at 16/17 tonnes GVW. The 1900 was produced to compete with the lighter models in this weight category. A restyled cab front common to all DAFs was introduced at the same time.

The new lightweight 1900 chassis became popular for many uses and the giant Pickford company took on the model as the basis of large removal vans. In this configuration they performed adequately, but did not like a headwind.

Ramage Bros. was a Lanarkshire distribution company that worked in the white goods delivery sector. The DAF 1900 was taken on by them as a large box van for their local delivery work.

Also given a face-lift and a higher powered engine was the middleweight range, which became the 2500. This particular truck operated in the Channel Island of Jersey, where width and weight restrictions curtailed large trucks to this size.

The 2500 was seen as an ideal drawbar unit where gross weights were not at the maximum capacity. A large retail chain used this 2500 on trunk haulage, with demountable bodies for local distribution.

DAFs were not seen in any quantity with the UK fire brigades. The 2500 range would probably have made an ideal fire appliance, with a good power to weight ratio, but Scania and Volvo were the preferred types when Kent Fire Brigade commissioned this one.

DAF also produced lightweight trucks using the 1700 designation. They were for gross weights up to 14 tonnes and had small wheels, making low loading heights for distribution work. Only a few were sold in the UK as they did not compete in price with the likes of IVECO, Renault and Leyland.

The older 2300 model was seen as a good 24-tonne tipper chassis; however, by the time this one was new, a move to higher weight 4-axle tippers at 32 tonnes was evident. DAF competed in the 4-axle tipper market most ably.

The 2100 model was still available and could be used as a drawbar unit for lighter loads. This one worked on contract to Westermann, hauling motor parts around the European car makers.

A further upgrade saw the 2500 models becoming the 2700, also with the new corporate front panels. When this truck was new the merger with Leyland had taken place, and for a time DAFs and Leylands were badged as Leyland DAFs.

An intermediate model with 3200 badging was introduced, using the high and wide cab, in the lead-up to the introduction of the new 95 range, and was a precursor of the later 85XF types. Inter-City Transport, a member of the Transport Development Group (TDG), used this one.

The new 95 range was introduced in the mid-1980s, with a new style of cab designed by Cab-Tech, and also used by Seddon-Atkinson and Pegaso. This cab gave the 95 range an imposing look and was considered a great working place, with good visibility and driver comfort.

In the course of time, the 95 range was converted by users to suit their purposes, and North Eastern Bus Breakers extended this one to suit their business. When the 95 range was introduced in the UK, they carried the Leyland DAF name.

This is an early Leyland DAF 95, then in the fledgling fleet of Billy Bowie – an Ayrshire waste disposal operator. It is notable as one of a few of this type that were seen with a 'day cab', which gives it a slightly unusual appearance. (A. Syme)

In keeping with the earlier 3300/3600 heavyweight tractor units, the new 95 range incorporated heavy tractors. This VVS of Leeds, a 95 with a large digging machine body, was waiting for a police escort.

An early Leyland DAF 95, which has long ago seen the first flush of life, being used as a vintage vehicle transporter – a job it would be well on top of.

The 95 range was basically intended as an artic unit for 38 tonnes in the UK. This caravan transporter would also be well on top of its job, with power to spare.

A straightforward Leyland DAF 95 with a curtainside trailer running at 38 tonnes from the north-east of Scotland. It has been lettered in a rather old-fashioned style compared with the trailer, while the driver has added numerous personal adornments.

Another early Leyland DAF 95 unit from the north-east of Scotland in the traditional style of livery, this time with a refrigerated van. The 95 became a very popular artic unit with Scottish fridge operators.

D. R. Macleod, of Stornoway, ran a large fleet of lorries and vans, although DAFs were outnumbered by Scania. The Leyland DAF 95 seen here at Ballinluig, on the A9, is carrying a heavy haulage trailer, which was probably easier to transport as a load than towing it.

Once again, the big Leyland DAF heavy haulage type could be specified in the 95 range, and this one, in use by Heanor Haulage, has a usefully high rating in STGO Cat 2. It is waiting at Carlisle truck stop for an onward police escort.

This is a haulage model of the 95 range – but using a small trailer well below its maximum capacity of 38 tonnes – bringing vintage tractors to the National Tractor Club's annual road run, taking place that year around Ayrshire.

James Hope of Carlisle had this heavy haulage artic unit in 1989 rated for the top sector of STGO use, pulling a 4-axle low loader with a weight spreader dolly at the front. It was waiting for the police escort seen alongside.

At the time of the photograph, this 95 would be running at 38 tonnes and taking advantage of the lower road tax afforded by the use of 6 axles. The driver was having a break at the Carlisle truck stop.

Carlisle haulier R. W. Green had his Leyland DAF 95 on tipper work at 38 tonnes. Green was a small fleet operator and the 95 is seen parked beside his M.A.N.

Standing in the Carlisle truck stop are a Seddon-Atkinson Strato and a Leyland DAF 95, showing the similarity of the cabs. The basic cab is the same, with different front panels. S-A was first to use the high-roof version.

In the late 1980s, DAF took over the ailing British Leyland truck-building operation. The then range of Leyland lorries were rebadged as Leyland DAFs and were given new designations, and a front panel taking on the appearance of the current DAF models.

Leyland Roadtrain types became the Leyland DAF 80 and continued to be sold as such until the new DAF 85 range made its appearance.

The Leyland Constructors were designated the 80 range, and remained in production before the new 85 range was introduced.

Leyland Freighters were re-designated as the 50 and 60 models, depending on gross weight. The larger Freighters were equipped with DAF engines.

The lightweight Leyland Roadrunner had been sold by DAF in Holland prior to the merger, and was a popular truck in the UK. It was retained as the Leyland DAF 45.

Subsequently, the DAF range reverted to being known purely as DAF. Tom Bolland's good-looking 95 shows the DAF-only badging, which had continued on trucks not intended for the UK.

A Dutch 95 seen having a break in the Carlisle truck stop with a rather unusual load, which might have been a mast for a sailing craft.

The original John Miller of Dumfries fleet was turned out in a fairly simple white and blue colour scheme, and kept in clean condition. The driver has added some adornment to brighten up the livery of his Leyland DAF.

The DAF 65, 75, and 85 range was introduced in the early 1990s as medium to heavyweight lorries, ranging from 13 tonnes up to 44 tonnes. This Hoddam Contracting Co. tipper was an early model, carrying the Leyland DAF name, and was a 26-tonner.

The heavier 95 range could be specified as a drawbar unit and Blighline had several as transport for their retail equipment supply business. The truck and trailer are fitted with TIR-style bodies for European work.

The 95 range continued to be well-favoured by fridge operators and this one, in use by an own-account meat wholesaler, is set up for 44 tonnes, and has a typical Scottish scene on the side, depicting the origin of the load carried.

Haulage Services, of Belfast, run a tidy fleet and their Leyland DAF was no exception. The majority of the 95 models at this time were fitted with 380 bhp DAF engines – descendants of the Leyland 0.680 diesel unit.

A DAF 95 in the north of England, but from Holland. It has refrigeration on the truck and trailer incorporated within the bodywork, which is not normally seen in the UK. It also has a cab-top sleeper pod, which cannot be comfortable, particularly if the refrigeration unit needs to run.

Luce Bay Plant Hire seems an unlikely user of a livestock lorry, but the owner was a farmer and cattle dealer. The Leyland DAF 95 could be put to various uses, with platform and construction trailers.

Leyland DAF marketed the 85 model generally as a 4-axle type suitable for tipper use, and many were to be seen in use by quarry and roadstone companies. RMC operated this early 300 bhp model in the north of England.

Scottish Premier Beef, seen in an earlier picture, also ran the Leyland DAF 75 type on long-distance distribution. At 300 bhp, this type was quite an impressive performer. An 85 model, with a larger engine, was available.

The Leyland DAF 85 was a lighter-weight artic unit than the 95 and was expected to perform at 38 tonnes, and later at higher weights. With the lower and smaller cab, it was useful in places where access was tight. Apart from the model designation, it had a deeper headlamp panel to accommodate a slightly raised cab over the larger engine it had fitted.

The Leyland DAF 65 catered for the 17-tonne and under gross weight range, effectively superseding the older Leyland models. It was a popular truck, in van and refrigerated form, for local distribution. This one may have been fitted out as a local radio outside broadcast van later in life.

John Miller Transport also ran the 85 range as artics with the 380 bhp engine. The 85 cab, being fitted lower on the chassis, had a fairly large engine cover in the cab, making access a little awkward to the sleeper compartment, but no worse than its contemporary Volvos and Scanias.

A minority of the Leyland DAF 85 tipper models ran with specialist equipment and this one has a liquid waste disposal tanker. It was 'doing its business' at a Cumbria Steam Gathering on a hot summer day, which kept it free of people, allowing a good clear shot for the camera!

R. Swain & Sons are well-known Kentish hauliers who stuck to a particular type of lorry.
Leyland were the mainstay for many years, and now the majority of the fleet is provided by
DAFs. The fleet livery and lettering have been a tradition for many years.

As earlier mentioned, the Leyland DAF 65 was a useful distribution lorry and this one,
loaded with potatoes, would be doing such work. With a 210 bhp engine, it would be
adequately powered at 17 tonnes gross.

The Transport Development Group (TDG) was a large corporate company, where economy of operation was the byword, and therefore a no-frills outlook was reflected on vehicle specifications. This Leyland DAF 85 was a fleet standard. The TDG was incorporated into the giant French Norbert Dentressangle operation.

The 270 bhp Leyland DAF 75 was a useful tipper at 26 tonnes gross. This truck for D. H. Kinder, of Cheadle, is fitted with a high-sided tipper body for coal haulage. (B. Tuck)

A livestock lorry with a third, or pusher axle, on a 75 range chassis. It is a factory built 6-wheeler, with a gross weight of 23 tonnes, rather than an after-market conversion. It has a 300 bhp engine.

The Leyland DAF 65 could be ordered from a long list of wheelbases and this baker's van seems to be on the longest, allowing a very large van body for the bakery products.

RMC used a large number of the Leyland DAF 75 range as 3-axle tippers. This one has an insulated tipper body for the carriage of hot tarmacadam, and worked in the north of England, in Cumbria.

John Raymond Transport was, until recently, a large fleet based in south Wales. It operated a diverse fleet and used various types of DAF trucks. The well-used Leyland DAF 85 pictured is typical of the fleet. (P. Crang)

Kilmarnock Removals have featured earlier in this book, using a DAF 3300. A later intake into the small fleet was this Leyland DAF 65 with a cab-top sleeper pod, allowing for a longer removal van body. The drivers would have found it well down on power after the bigger 3300.

Hayton Coulthard Ltd is one of the larger fleets operating in the Scottish Dumfries and Galloway area. This Leyland DAF 85 carries the traditional Coulthard livery, but may have belonged to a sub-contractor.

A drawbar outfit based on a Leyland DAF 75 chassis in the premises of the Carlisle DAF dealership. The loads must have been light, or the heavier 85 chassis would have been specified.

This Leyland DAF 85 with the 330 bhp engine was brand new and had not gone to work at the time of the photograph. It was operated in agricultural and livestock transport around the markets in southern Scotland. This particular traditional livery has been seen on the road for many years.

Midlothian Council had a number of snowplough and gritter trucks based on the 270 bhp Leyland DAF 75 chassis. This one was new and in the premises of the Edinburgh DAF dealership, awaiting delivery to a contractor for the council.

Stalker's Transport, of Carlisle, was a staunch supporter of the DAF marque and this 85 type is one of many in the fleet. It has a second steering axle, allowing it to run at 38 tonnes gross.

In the later 1990s, the Leyland name disappeared from the front of Leyland DAFS. The small Roadrunner was the only original Leyland in production, so it seemed logical to return to the DAF name for DAF designs. The 95XF was the next evolution of the type.

The DAF 75 range came in for the same badging, as seen on this tipper operated by Denny Tipper Transport, and is seen attending a Scottish Truckfest as a working lorry, rather than an exhibit.

Many DAF 85 artic units were converted in the south of Scotland to useful long wheelbase trucks after they had been used by national distribution fleets and written down in value. This fresh-looking truck may have been such a conversion.

G. W. Holliday of Penrith always presented a neat and tidy fleet. In latter days, the fleet contained DAFs, with this Leyland DAF 85 being typical.

The Leyland DAF 55 was a carry-over of the former Leyland 17-tonner, which had its origins in Leyland and Albion chassis. It was a cheaper alternative to the DAF 65 and was often found in council or road engineering fleets. It used the original T45 cab design of the 1980s.

Sam Ostle ran a fleet of DAFS that were said to be exchanged at very short intervals, and therefore were in high demand by second users. This 85CF was used on general haulage. Sam Ostle was absorbed by Turners of Soham in recent times.

Small rigid car transporters are a fairly rare commodity due to the lesser numbers of cars that can be carried. Arnold Clark, the nationwide car dealer, used this 75 chassis, with an additional weight spreading axle, to move cars the short distances between their outlets.

The lower and smaller 85 cab was found to be a better type for fuel tankers that had to access restricted filling station forecourts. The height of the cab usually matched the top of the tanker trailer, making for good aerodynamics. Fuel companies always wanted cost-effectiveness!

The name of Stamper has always been connected with transport in Cumbria. Mike Stamper ran this DAF 85CF on brick and block transport. Other members of the Stamper haulage clan were prolific DAF users.

Found at a vintage vehicle rally was this DAF 65 on a long wheelbase and adapted with a beaver tail for loading over the rear end. It has been adorned by a superb graphic of a Field Marshal tractor, which it no doubt transported.

On the Channel Island of Jersey the Channel Express importing and exporting company used this DAF 85. It carries some sort of permit notice, which may allow it to run on the Jersey roads at 30 tonnes gross.

The original Leyland Roadrunner evolved into the DAF 45 and was retained as the DAF model for the 7.5-tonne market. This one has a particularly large box van for local deliveries.

One of the former well-known Reid's Transport DAF 95XF artics is about to take on a very large concrete pipe from a ship docked at Ayr harbour. Reid's Transport was essentially a tipper operator, and this would be an on-off job.

Ecclefechan is a small village, at one time on the A74 road – the name well-known as a measure of sobriety. The Ecclefechan Coal Company use this good-looking DAF 95XF with a small-wheeled third axle conversion.

The DAF 85CF was always a popular 8-wheel tipper. D. S. Denham operated a few alongside other makes, and a direct comparison can be made with the Foden cab alongside, which is a modified DAF unit, fitted to Fodens after rationalisation by the parent Paccar company.

The DAF 65 could be specified down to 13/14 tonnes gross, but only a few appeared in the UK. This small Dutch-registered DAF 65, working in Amsterdam, gives an idea of the model, which looks strange on its small wheels,

The DAF 75CF made a compact domestic fuel tanker and, when fitted with a steering tag-axle, as here, the manoeuvrability would have been very good in tight places such as house drives and farms. (K. Durston)

Reid's Transport used this Leyland DAF 85 on internal transport within Ayr Docks, moving silica sand from ships to storage. It is a high ground-clearance model, with straight front axles, lifting the chassis frame and the cab out of harm's way.

In the north-east of England, Teward Bros. run a fleet of tippers with a strong contingent of DAFs. Shown here are consecutive models illustrating changes to the frontal appearance.

In the early 2000s, DAF tied in with Renault and Volvo to utilise a new cab for all their lightweight trucks. The cab was fitted to DAFs from the 45 7.5-tonner to the 55 17/18-tonners. It was by no means spacious!

The straight beam front axles are seen to effect on this DAF 85CF, showing how they raise
the front of the chassis and the cab – very effective in eliminating damage on sites, but it
gives a long climb in and out for the driver.

A DAF 55LF in the Christian Salvesen livery doing deliveries on Edinburgh's High Street,
better known as the Royal Mile. This was photographed around the time when Salvesen
was taken over by Norbert Dentressangle and disappeared from the transport scene.

A DAF 75 with a drawbar trailer having a break near the M74 one summer's day. The operating company is described as healthcare specialists, and the trailer has refrigeration. Whatever the load is, it can't be heavy with only a need for four axles.

The DAF 75 is a good base for livestock haulage. The F. Davidson fleet of around fifteen is all-DAF with a mixture of 75 and 85 types as rigid trucks, and a number of 95XF artic with double-deck livestock trailers.

Reid's Transport used the medium-height cab on the DAF 95XF models for extra driver
accommodation, but being tippers could not use the higher cab because of height issues in
farms and factories.

The DAF cabs have been uprated gradually since they were first introduced, with the larger
cab having been around from the early 1990s. Transam Trucking use this 105XF DAF
in the international movement of pop artist shows, where the extended rearwards and
upwards accommodation is a boon to the drivers.

Campbell's DAF 95XF was specified with the medium-height cab for the same reasons as at Reid's Transport. It is fitted with a 430 bhp engine, which is considered as average power.

A third DAF 95XF artic tipper, with the medium-height cab. P. Hinchcliffe had a medium-sized fleet of tippers and general haulage artics, where DAFs were a minority among Scanias. The company closed some years ago.

Irish companies have been enthusiastic operators of DAFs since they became available
in the UK. This 95XF and trailer looked new and is carrying a substantial load of new
agricultural equipment.

The larger DAFs were taken up readily by recovery companies, and this 95XF in the
colours of Ian Gordon Commercials was extended and fitted with bespoke recovery gear to
the owner's specifications.

T. P. Niven started out as a small agricultural haulier in the south of Scotland, on milk churn transport. Development of the firm in recent times has seen the fleet grow, retaining milk transport, with general and contract haulage for national companies. The DAF 85Cf is used on local deliveries on behalf of Palletline.

Another version of the DAF 75 on domestic and farm fuel deliveries. This one is probably a 6x4, or maybe a 6x2. Farmers do not like a 6x4 type as they claim the tyre scrub rips up their roads and farmyards.

This is an older Leyland DAF, badged 75, in use in Northern Ireland as a transit concrete mixer. It looks to be well-maintained and kept clean – something hard to do with a mixer truck.

Brand-new, and probably still to go into service, was this DAF 85CF on a very wet day in the Cumbrian countryside. The DAF and trailer have six axles between them and it would be used at 44 tonnes gross.

Two very smart DAF 95XF artic units entered in a small truck show at Penrith. They have a higher version of the medium cab, evolved to allow more internal height.

The DAF 105XF has a much larger cab and can be identified by the built-in headlamps in the front of the roof. Even with the extra lights on the vehicle the owner has fitted aftermarket light bars, which must give tremendous forward vision in the dark.

Tom French & Son took over the business of Reid's Transport, introducing DAFs to an otherwise all-Volvo fleet. The 95XF is seen with a standard French tipping trailer for grain transport. French has not been converted away from Volvos.

Another DAF in an otherwise Volvo fleet. R. & A. Muir ran Albions for many years, followed by Leylands and Volvos. This DAF 75CF concrete mixer works locally to the operating base in central Ayrshire.

The mainly white fleet of Noel Zwecker, from Northern Ireland, was always a mixture of makes. The DAF 95XF with a Super Space cab was one of the last trucks operated by the company before closure.

A DAF 85CF concrete mixer, in the west of Scotland Breedon fleet, is shown to advantage against a spring background. Breedon has embarked on quarry company take-overs around Scotland in recent years. The DAF would have been previously operated by Barr Construction.

Tyson H. Burridge was well-known as a buyer and refurbisher of Seddon-Atkinsons for his fleet. The DAF 85CF has since become the mainstay of this Cumbrian fleet – well finished in two-tone blue, with clear signwriting.

The small 7.5-tonne DAF 45LF sells well due to its light weight, giving a decent load allowance over its competitors. This one carries specialist equipment for clearing toilets at public events.

The heavier version of the LF models, a 55, in service with Stocks & Sons of Cornwall. There are not many 2-axle heavyweight tippers nowadays. Stocks are renowned for their fleet care, and having used some unusual types. (P. Crang)

Gregory Distribution is a long-term operator from the West Country. This DAF XF is one regularly seen in Scotland since a merger with Hayton Coulthard Transport.

The DAF 75CF seen here was part of a small tipper fleet operating in and around Penrith in Cumbria. The owners were keen on truckshows and that is reflected in the way their lorries were kept.

The DAF 75CF was often used as a base for transit concrete mixers, and this Northern Ireland machine gives an almost profile picture of the layout. While by no means in pristine condition, it seems to be kept clean except for road dirt.

Glasgow Council operated a large number of DAF75CF trucks as refuse collectors on short wheelbases. The wheelbases on some are almost of artic unit dimensions, and the rear loading hopper gives them a tail-heavy appearance.

Operators have found the DAF 55LF eminently suitable as a skip loader. The narrow cab allows far better access to premises than the larger 65CF cab, while the truck is lighter and less expensive than its stablemate.

Barr Quarries ran DAF 85CF 8-wheel tippers for a long time, alongside the 75 6-wheel version. This one highlights the number of mirrors fitted to heavy trucks in this day and age. (E. Waugh)

Robert Summers has been for a long time a Mercedes-Benz operator, but in recent times has turned to DAF. Their DAF 95XF, *Kingdom Hurricane*, is seen returning to base after delivering a load of timber trusses.

In 2008, this DAF 85CF was new and an exhibit on the DAF sales area at the Scottish Truckfest that summer. It is another high ground-clearance model, destined for difficult off-road work.

Two 95XF DAFs, which made up the majority of the Reid's Transport fleet. The traditional image was applied to the trucks in this fleet by a combination of vinyl and signwriting. The fleet worked throughout the UK and Eire.

The Jamieson family are farmers and haulage contractors. This DAF 105XF was acquired with a double-deck livestock trailer because of the distance from their operating area to the nearest regular market. It has the 510 bhp engine.

One of the last DAFs in the Reid's Transport fleet was this 85CF, with high ground clearance. It moved on with the sale of the business to Tom French & Son. It is an impressive truck with its high-sided bulk body and almost matching height cab.

The excellent Pollock Scotrans livery is seen all over the UK on artic curtainsiders, while a smaller fleet of distribution lorries can be found working in the Scottish cities. Equipped with a low-height sleeper cab, the DAF 65 types have not been skimped on with the application of the livery.

A skip loader on the DAF 45LF 7.5-tonne chassis. Ideal for delivering large skips, as seen here, but it would only have been able to lift loaded midi-skips as suggested on the lettering.

This DAF 85CF 8-wheel bulk tipper is a world away from the skip loader in the previous picture, with a gross weight of 32 tonnes. It wears an attractive livery style, telling all and sundry it is carrying wood chip and pellets – an alternative energy source.

In the same vein, this DAF 45LF is almost a traditional coalman's lorry if it wasn't for the curtainside body. As the operator is also a builder's merchant, the curtains would give other materials protection from the weather. It was a DAF exhibit at the 2009 Scottish Truckfest.

In a livery style designed to catch the eye, this DAF 55LF is operated by Kilmarnock Removals, as seen elsewhere in the book, but under different management. Since the photograph was taken, Kilmarnock Removals have reverted to a stylised yellow and blue colour scheme.

The late John Alexander had two DAF 85CF tippers. This one, registered in 2009, has been kept in very good condition, considering the work it was put to.

A big DAF 85CF with drain clearing equipment about to go to work on Brighton's Madeira Drive. It has a 410 bhp engine, which would be an advantage in powering the pumping equipment.

The DAF 75CF artic unit had become a rare beast when Kuhene & Nagel placed this one on contract to the Waitrose supermarket chain. Making it doubly rare is the so-called day cab and its 310 bhp engine, which will make it unattractive to second life users.

Bullet Express runs this DAF 85CF moving aircraft components to and from the aviation industry around Prestwick Airport. Larger DAF 95s or 105XFs are used with long trailers to move wing parts under abnormal load conditions.

The DAF 55LF can be specified with three axles and smaller wheels, allowing a long and low load platform favoured by the brewery trade. This one, on Edinburgh's Royal Mile, has single wheels on the third axle, suggesting that it steers to cut down on tyre scrub.

The DAF55LF in domestic fuel tanker form is a compact and highly manoeuvrable little vehicle, with the agility to enter farms and house driveways with tight access.

The most recent DAF 75CF trucks are almost identical in looks to the heavier 85CF types. The recognition factor for the 75CF is still the shallower headlight panel.

W. H. McWilliam operates from the south of Scotland with a growing fleet, most of which are DAF trucks. The minimalist livery applied to this 105XF harks back to the operator's traditional style, without painting the cab overall.

Carrying an agricultural cropping machine will be well inside the capabilities of this DAF 105XF. It displays a Category 2 STGO plate and could gross up to 80 tonnes.

Pollock Scotrans used this 95XF on trunk haulage. In keeping with their tradition of naming trucks after current events, films, and TV programmes, the DAF carries the fleet name *Avatar*.

Brand new and awaiting delivery to its owner is this DAF 85CF, with a 510 bhp engine, giving plenty of power to run with a trailer at 44 tons gross.

The Quinn Group from Northern Ireland have a daily delivery of cement into Scotland. This DAF 85CF is returning for a ferry crossing home.

Another DAF 85CF running to the Northern Ireland ferries from its Scottish base. It has been extensively fitted with air management equipment, which along with a fairly lightweight load should afford good fuel consumption.

A DAF 85CF working in Edinburgh delivering domestic fuel, and seen passing the foot of Calton Hill, at the Scottish Government Office, on Regent Road.

McClellan Transport operates this DAF 105XF on refrigerated transport. It has been fitted with an enlarged fuel tank to increase its range, and an additional axle with small wheels to allow it to run at 44 tonnes.

A similar set-up can be seen in this DAF 105XF operated on general haulage by Maxwell Freight Services, of Northern Ireland. It is travelling to the Irish ferry terminals in the south-west of Scotland.

MKT Trucking, of Lancashire, is part of the pop concert transport group of operators and had this DAF105XF, and others, on concert venue haulage. It was parked awaiting its next move outside such a venue in Glasgow.

Reliable Trucking is a sub-contractor to Hayton Coulthard Transport. Their DAF 105XF is seen in an M6 service station refuelling. Hayton Coulthard trucks are usually named, with this one known as *Bethany's Pride* – a reference to a wife, or daughter.

Continuing in the theatrical haulage theme, EST (Edwin Shirley Trucking) is one of the better-known names. Two of their DAF 105XF artics are seen here at the Scottish Exhibition Centre in Glasgow.

A W. H. McWilliam truck has featured elsewhere in this book. Here is one of their latest DAFs, a 105XF with the 510 bhp engine working on general haulage in Ayrshire.

Pollock Scotrans have this DAF 105XF with a 440 bhp engine, no doubt for well thought out logistical reasons. The traditional livery bears the usual tartan sash with the fleet name *Wee Jock* – perhaps a reference to the driver.

A DAF 85CF with a high-roof cab making its way south on the A77 trunk road to Stranraer. A general haulage truck, becoming a rarity with a platform trailer, it may be heading for Northern Ireland to collect farm machinery, or concrete product, both commodities of which are regularly hauled from the province.

DAF marketed a bonneted range of trucks but they were never offered for sale in the UK. There is a small market for bonneted trucks, which are mainly converted forward-control types. This is how a DAF looks, given the conversion treatment. Beauty is in the eye of the beholder!